Water Polo Explained

Andy Stein

Water Polo Explained

Andy Stein

**Reviewed by Gary Tonks,
ex-GB International Water Polo player**

ISBN 978-1-79650-350-0

Published 2019 by Andy Stein. First published as an ebook in 2018.

Contents

Preface

This book has been written for new water polo players (and their families), new referees and anyone else who takes an interest in this great sport. I wrote it initially so I could understand the many rules, and later to help me pass a referee's examination.

Some say water polo is a bit like 'underwater rugby' (one of the original names was 'aquatic football'). But, I would argue, as an ex-rugby player, that it is a better game. Whether better or not, there are many more goals, no scrums/line outs which slow down the game, and many less injuries. It is fast, furious and rough – with beers after the game. And you can keep playing all your life. Quite a few rules changes were announced by FINA (the governing body for water sports) in 2019. These have been incorporated in the book.

Please email me at a.stein538@btinternet.com if you have any comments or suggestions about this book. Thank you.

Acknowledgements

I would like to thank Mike Pagan, Gordon Young, Quentin Hayes, Duncan Holland and Mark Baxter for making me so welcome at Warwick Water Polo Club when I started playing in 2017.

I am also very grateful to three reviewers. The senior reviewer is Gary Tonks, an ex-Great Britain international and still playing for Boldmere 1st team (in Sutton Coldfield). He is a great player, coach, referee, and a 'Mr Water Polo' in the Midlands of the UK – and a great guy. Brian Pugh (Walsall Club) has also added useful comments.

The second reviewer is Gordon Young, who is an experienced Warwick player and referee. As a fellow club member, he has had to endure my play (and decisions as referee). They have (and do) put up with me regularly catching the ball with two hands, jumping up in the shallow end and tackling over-enthusiastically. The third reviewer is Yiannis Giannouris, an ex-Greece international and national coach for Greece. He added comments on the first chapter on the history of the sport, of which he is a expert.

I would also like to thank Stephen Theaker for his help in producing the ebook, and for his patience when I asked him to re-set the print version of the book to include the 2019 FINA rule changes.

Most importantly, I would like to thank my wife, Emma, and children, Poppy (also a water polo player) and Isaac, for putting up with me. A 'water polo life' means endless trips to the pool; refereeing late in the evening, talking too much about the game, and trunks, goggles, towels and water polo balls left all over the house.

Chapter One:
Introduction and History

Water Polo is best described as a combination of swimming, rugby and handball. It is an international team sport. Skills include swimming, eye/hand co-ordination (as only one hand can be used to pass or throw), and wrestling.

The game originated as a form of rugby football played in rivers and lakes in England and Scotland with a ball constructed of Indian rubber, probably from the 1850s onwards. This 'water rugby' came to be called 'water polo' based on the English pronunciation of the Balti (Tibetan language of Kashmir) word pulu, which means 'ball'.

1850–70s

In the first edition (1893) of their book Swimming, Archibald Sinclair and William Henry state "On May 12, 1870, a committee was appointed by the Swimming Association, then known as the London Swimming Association, to draw up a code of rules for the management of the game of 'football in the water'." This indicates that forms of the sport we now call 'water polo' existed before the current name was in common use. Other names included 'water base ball' and (more frequently) 'aquatic football'. For example, in the South Eastern Gazette (in Kent; now closed), on Tues 28th July 1857, it says "An aquatic foot-ball match is fixed for to-morrow, Wednesday". This was in a piece about Maidstone Swimming Club, which was founded in 1844, and is possibly the oldest club in the world.

One of the earliest recorded games of a sport called 'water polo' occurred at the Crystal Palace (London), on 15th September 1873. It was reported in the Morning Post (now closed) and The Standard (later London Evening Standard). The weather was "cold and raw" according the Penny Illustrated News. It was held in the boating lake that still exists. It was part of the 4th Open Air Fete of the London Swimming Club (founded in 1859).

On 13th July 1876, near to the midpoint of Bournemouth Pier, there was a game between 12 members[1] of the Premier Rowing Club – with goals being marked by four flags placed in the water. The game started at 6pm in the evening and lasted for 15 minutes (when the ball burst), and was watched by a large crowd; with plans being made for play on a larger scale the following week.

On 26th September 1877, the second gala of the Tyldesley (near Wigan) Swimming Club took place. A poster of this event survives and mentions a "Great Game of Water Polo, two games out of three (between) Mr Roscoe's and Mr Walshaw's side".

The modern game also developed in Scotland in the late 19th century, when the first games of water polo were played at the Arlington Baths Club[2] in Glasgow (the Club was founded in 1870, and still exists today). In 1886, the Scottish Amateur Swimming Association (Western) held their first championship, the West Cup. West of Scotland beat South Side 1-0. This is probably the first club tournament in the world, and is still played for today.

Another version of a common set of rules appeared in 1877, when the President of the Bon Accord

---

[1] For the record, these are some of the players that took part in that game: OC Mootham, WJ and E Worth, FT Cutler, H Nash, H Harvey and JA Nethercoate.

[2] The first municipal pool in the UK was St George's Baths (salt-water) at Pier Head in Liverpool, founded in 1828.

Swimming Club, William Wilson (Figure 1 below), probably the first Baths Master of 'the Arlington', requested that the President of the Associated Swimming Clubs of Scotland (ASCS) recommend a way to increase interest in the club's annual gala. He created, from start to finish, a set of rules for a game called 'aquatic football'.

Figure 1: William Wilson (1844 - 1912): Scottish swimming and water polo pioneer

1880s–1900

The Swimming Association of Great Britain (SAGB; forerunner of the Amateur Swimming Association, of England)[3] recognised the sport on 13th April 1885.

Canada was one of the first countries outside the United Kingdom to adopt the sport. The Montreal Swimming Club formed in 1876, with a water polo team starting in 1887. In 1888, the sport was brought to the USA, by John Robinson, an English swimming

[3] Previously Associated Metropolitan Swimming Clubs (AMSC, founded 7th January 1869), then London Swimming Association (LSA; 1869), then Metropolitan Swimming Association (MSA; 1870), then Swimming Association of Great Britain (SAGB; 1873), then Amateur Swimming Association (ASA, 1886).

instructor; by organising a team at the Boston Athletic Association. Two years later, J.H. Smith and Arnold Heilban started a team at the Sydenham Swimmers Club (later at the Metropole AC) in Providence, Rhode Island. In the autumn of the same year (1890) the New York Athletic Club (NYAC) introduced the game to members. The first US championships were held on 28th January 1890, in Providence, when Sydenham Swimmers Club defeated Boston Athletic Association by 2:1. Water polo spread to Hungary in 1889, Belgium in 1890, Austria and Germany in 1894 and France in 1895.

The Midland (of England) Counties Swimming and Aquatic Football Association[4] probably set up the first water polo league in the world. Their first champions, in 1884, were Birmingham Leander who beat Hanley 1–0.

The first national club championships (in England) were played in 1888. Burton Amateur Club defeated Otter Swimming Club 3–0 in the Old Lambert Baths in London. Burton Amateur was formed in 1878, and still exists today. Otter was formed in London in 1869; and also still exists today, with male and female water water polo teams. Though originally it was a male-only swimming club.

The London Water Polo League, encouraged by the Otter Club, was formed in 1889. In that year, Nautilus were the first champions, defeating Otter 2–0. The next league was the Northern Counties. Their first champions were Manchester Osborne, who beat Manchester Leaf Street 4–1, in 1892. The longest running single match is the annual one between Oxford and Cambridge universities. This first one was

[4] Midland Counties was founded on 20th May, 1884, in Burton-on-Trent. It published their version of the rules of water polo. In 1895, eight clubs, within ten miles of Birmingham, founded the Birmingham & District Water Polo League (BDWPL). The BDWPL was one of the original groups of clubs to form the British Water Polo League (BWPL) on 1st December 1962; along with Birkenhead, Cheltenham, Otter (London), Polytechnic (London), Sheffield Dolphins, Sutton & Cheam and Weston-super-Mare.

played on October 16th 1891, at the Old Crown Baths, Kensington Oval, London. Oxford won 4-1.

The first international water polo match was between England and Scotland at the Kensington Baths in London, on July 28th, 1890. Scotland won 4-0. The England team were F Browne, WG Carrey, HF Clark, JF Genders, William Henry, J Finegan and JL Mayger. The referee was Archibald Sinclair (1866-1922; who also founded the London Water Polo league) from Ranelagh Harriers, England. William Henry[5] (1859-1928) and Archibald Sinclair went on to publish a book called Swimming (Longmans & Co, London) in 1893. It included a chapter on water polo and may be the first book to have a chapter on the subject.

Things (and rules) change in water polo. For example, in the early years of the sport, goalkeepers were would stand on the edge of a the pool, as shown in figure 2 (below).

Figure 2: Early goalkeepers stood on the edge of the pool

---

[5] William Henry (born Joseph Nawrocki, and of Polish descent) was a prolific swimmer, who also held multiple national swimming titles.

Womens' Water Polo

Womens' water polo is not new. Figure 3 (below) shows a women's water polo match between Jersey and Swansea; in the final of the Ravensbourne Challenge Shield at the Westminster Baths in London, on October 6th 1900.

Figure 3: Early womens' water polo. Jersey vs Swansea, Ravensbourne Challenge Shield final, 1900.

Olympic History

Water polo (for men) was one of the five original team sports[6] chosen for the Olympics in Paris in 1900 (the second games of the Modern Era), and has been an Olympic sport since then. There were no team sports in the 1896 games in Athens. Great Britain have won the gold medal four times, in 1900, 1908, 1912 and 1920. In 1904 (in St Louis, Missouri) water polo was a demonstration sport, and only the USA competed.

In the Paris Olympics, the final was held in the River Seine, on August 12th, between Great Britain and Belgium. The GB players were: Thomas Coe,

[6] For the record, the five were: water polo, rugby union, football (soccer), polo and tug-of-war.

Robert Crawshaw, William Henry,[7] John Arthur Jarvis, Peter Kemp, Victor Lindberg and Frederick Stapleton. GB won 7–2. Figure 4 is taken from the 1908 Olympics in London.

Figure 4: Water polo. London Olympics, 1908.

There was also a womens' exhibition game (not for medals) between two Dutch teams (from Amsterdam and Rotterdam) at the 1920 Olympic Games in Antwerp (see Figure 5 below).

Figure 5: Womens' Exhibition match, at Antwerp Olympics (1920)

Then there was a long wait until women's water polo became a full Olympic sport. This happened at

---

[7] This was another of William Henry's achievements, then aged 41 years.

the Sydney Games in 2000. This was in part secondary to daily protests staged by the Australian national water polo team during the 1999 IOC meeting in Melbourne.

So a women's competition was introduced 100 years after men's water polo was included in the Olympic programme. Australia won the gold medal match 4:3 against the United States with a 'buzzer-beating' last-minute goal, taken from outside the seven-metre line. Russia defeated the Netherlands for bronze 4–3.

GB women have only qualified once for the Olympics, in London, in 2012 – and came 8th. The players were Francesca Clayton, Lisa Gibson, Ciara Gibson-Byrne, Rebecca Kershaw, Frances Leighton, Fiona McCann, Rosemary Morris, Hazel Musgrove, Robyn Nicholls, Alexandra Rutlidge, Francesca Snell, Chloe Wilcox and Angela Winstanley-Smith.

In the same Olympics, GB men came 12th with the following team: Craig Figes, Matthew Holland, Ciaran James, Sean King, Joseph O'Regan, Robert Parker, Alexander Parsonage, Glen Robinson, Sean Ryder, Adam Scholefield, Edward Scott, Jake Vincent and Jack Waller.

It is a professional or semi-professional sport all over the world, notably in Europe (particularly in Hungary, Serbia, Croatia, Montenegro, Russia, Italy, Netherlands, Greece and Spain), the United States, Canada and Australia. Although, in the UK, it is entirely amateur. Hungary men have won more Olympic golds than any other country (eight). Serbia and USA are the current (2016) mens' and womens' champions, respectively. In women's Olympic water polo, the USA have most gold medals (two, at the London and Rio Olympics, in 2012 and 2016).

FINA (and its International competitions)

FINA or Fédération Internationale de Natation (International Swimming Federation) is the international federation recognised by the International Olympic Committee (IOC), which administers international competition in water sports. This includes water polo. It is based in Lausanne, Switzerland.

In 1911, the English-Scottish rules of the time became obligatory for all FINA member nations. Now FINA writes the rules of water polo,[8] which are updated regularly, often with the objective of speeding up the game. Their latest set of rules (2017–2021) were published in September 2017.

The first mens' World Water Polo Championships was held by FINA (the sport's governing body) in Belgrade (former Yugoslavia) in 1973. It occurs every two years (odd years). Croatia are the current (2017) champions. The first World Cup for men took place in 1979, also in Belgrade. It is also run by FINA, and occurs every four years. Hungary are the current (2018) champions.

FINA also organise a water polo World League. This is an international water polo league which plays annually, typically from winter to June. The top teams emerge to play in a championship tournament (the 'Super Final') where the league champion team is crowned. Montenegro are current (2018) champions. The first championship tournament, for men, was in Patras, Greece, in 2002.

The first Water Polo World Cup for women was held in 1979 in Merced, California. USA are current (2018) champions. The first Womens' World Championships took place in Madrid in 1986. USA are current (2017) champions. Both now occur at the same frequency as the men, ie every four and two years respectively. There is also an annual water polo World League for women. Its first championship (at the end of the season), was in 2004, in Long Beach, California. Again, USA are current (2018) champions.

---

[8] https://www.fina.org/content/water-polo-rules

Chapter Two:
Basics of Game

Water polo is a fierce, competitive and demanding game played over four, eight minute periods. Generally speaking, water polo is a simple game. The object is to work as a team to put the ball into the opposition team's net, scoring a goal.

The game clock is stopped when the ball is not in play; eg between an ordinary or exclusion foul being committed and a free throw being taken, or between a goal being scored and the restart, or after a corner or goal throw is awarded. As a result, the average quarter lasts around 12 minutes in real time, making 48 minutes in total.

Physical contact is the rule rather than the exception as players manoeuvre for position in front of the goal. There are 2 two minute intervals between time periods 1 and 2, and 3 and 4; with a five minute break at half time.[9] Players need to be fit, both aerobically and anaerobically.

Each coach (or captain if no coach is present) may request up to four timeouts, which are one minute in duration; but no more than one per quarter.[10] Their team must be in possession of the ball. The game is

[9] Note 2019 FINA rule change: Intervals between quarters. There will be a 3 minute interval between the second and third quarters, with a 2 minute interval between first and second, and third and fourth.

[10] Note 2019 FINA rule change: Timeouts. Each team may request 2 timeouts during the game at any time (ie they can be in the same quarter), except after the awarding of a penalty throw, by the coach of the team in possession of the ball.

then immediately stopped. If the defensive team calls a timeout, a penalty is awarded against them.

There is variation in timings at junior (and other) levels. For example, seven minute quarters are the norm. Also, the time between quarters 2 and 3 is less, usually two minutes. And there are two timeouts allowed. These can be taken at any time, ie up to two in one quarter.

The Team and Substitutions

Each team consists of a maximum of 13 players, seven players in the pool – a goalkeeper, and six outfield players. Due to the intense nature of the game, regular substitutions are common.

A player may be substituted at any time in the game by leaving the field of play, with the exception of when a referee awards a penalty.

Substitutions are most common after a goal is scored, between quarters, for an injured player, or during a timeout. A substitution is not allowed after a penalty has been awarded, but can take place after play has stopped after it (eg if a goal is scored).

At such times (ie when play is stopped) players may enter or exit anywhere. But during game play – when substitutions are not common – players (and substitutes) must exit and enter in their team's re-entry area. This can only happen after the substituted player is visible above water in the re-entry area.

The substitute must enter by ducking under the rope, without lifting it. If they do lift it, it can lead to an exclusion foul (see later) if their team is on the offensive (eg returning to pool after an exclusion foul if possession has changed), and a penalty (see later) if on defensive.

The Pool

The pool should be 25 metres (women) and 30 metres

(men) in length, and 20 metres wide, as shown in Figure 6. The goal is 3 metres wide, and 0.9-1.5 metres above the water. Ideally the pool should be 'all deep end' (1.8 metres deep), with players not being able to touch the bottom of the pool. In reality, many pools have a shallow end.

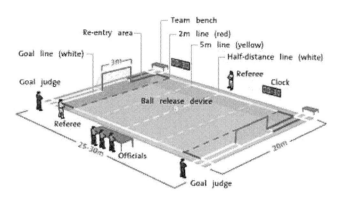

Figure 6. Water polo pool (international[11])

The goal and halfway line of the pool is designated by a white marker on both sides of the pool. There is also a 'five metre' line, where penalties are shot from, which is designated by a yellow marker.[12] And there is a 'two metre' line, designated by a red marker; no player of the attacking team can enter this area (unless you dribble the ball in), or receive a ball inside this zone. In some pools, there are 'yellow and red zones' marked on the side of the pool; instead of (or as well as) the markers (as in the picture above).

The area around the 2 metre line, in front of the goal, is often called the 'pit' or 'hole'. This is where the centre forward and centre back (see later) battle for possession of the ball, in front of the goalkeeper.

---

[11] Your local pool may look very different, shallow end, goals with holes in the net, and few officials!

[12] Note 2019 FINA rule change: A six metre line will now be added.

Object of the Game

One can push, carry or throw the ball into the goal to score a goal. If more goals are scored than the opposing team, this results in a win.

Players in possession of the ball can pass the ball forwards, sideways or backwards. Apart from a clenched fist, a goal may be scored by any part of the body.[13]

Players are only permitted to use one hand to hold the ball, apart from the goalkeeper who can use two hands when within 6 metres of the goal. So field players cannot use two hands to block a pass or shot.

Players are theoretically not allowed to touch the bottom of the pool. However, with shallow ends, this rule is hard to follow and referee. To show the referee you are at least attempting not to touch the bottom, it is important to keep at least one shoulder under the water (ie using a crab-like low stance, leaning to the right or left), especially when you shoot. Also jumping up in the shallow end is indicative of touching the bottom. If this rule is broken, an ordinary foul will be awarded against you (see later).

Unlike football (soccer), there is no real offside rule. Though offensive players cannot go into the 2 metre zone (eg to receive a pass when in the 2 metre zone) without the ball. So, a player can 'hang around' the 2 to 6 metre area, near the goal, if they want to; ie hoping for a long pass on a counter attack. This is sometimes called 'cherry picking'. This is not often done, as it will leave your team 'man-down' on defence.

Goals

A goal is scored when the entire ball passes fully over the goal line, between the goal posts and underneath the cross bar. A goal may be scored from any position

---

[13] You can kick the ball into the goal but not if it is reckless, and leads to kicking an opponent.

within the pool. A goal can also be scored directly from a free throw, if the shot is taken from outside 6 metres without delay. You are also allowed to dribble the ball in to the goal.

A goal can be awarded after the whistle to indicate the end of each period has occurred, if it was released before the whistle. But if the referee blows a whistle for a foul whilst the ball is in flight, a goal is not scored even it it goes across the goal line.

The referee signals a goal by a short whistle and immediately pointing to the centre of the field of play, with the arm angled down.

Winning the Game – Penalty Shoot-out

There is no overtime in water polo. So, at the end of a match, if a game is tied, and a result is required, a penalty shootout is used to determine the winner. A goalkeeper and five players are chosen by the coaches of each team. A player cannot be chosen if he/she is ineligible to play from receiving three personal fouls, or a game exclusion. Players shoot from the 5 metre line alternately at either end of the pool in turn, until all five have taken a shot. If the score is still tied, the same players shoot alternately until one team misses and the opposition scores.

Players and Equipment

Unlike other team games – such as football (soccer), rugby union, or hockey – where players have very specific positions to keep, water polo players move from position to position as the game demands. Nonetheless, there are positions, which are half-fixed, at least initially.

Positions are either offensive or defensive, with the offensive positions including: centre forward; two drivers (flats); two wings, who play on the flanks of the pool; and a point, who is positioned around the 5

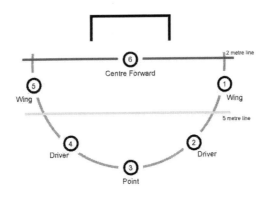

*Figure 7. The 'Arc' (standard offensive positions,
UK terminology)*

metre line. They often take up the positions in Figure 7, forming an 'arc'.

In terms of defensive positions, the only consistent roles are the goalkeeper and the centre back, whose job it is to mark the centre forward and steal the ball – and defend the goalkeeper and goal. Water polo positions are described in more detail in the next chapter.

Not much equipment is needed to play water polo. A net and a ball are required, and players wear simple swimsuits or trunks depending on sex, and swimming caps – usually white for the home team, and blue for the away team. The goalkeeper normally wears a red cap. The cap in water polo has two functions: (1) to protect the players' ears and heads; and (2) to make the player identifiable, especially by the referee(s) – as it has a number on it (1–13). Numbers 1 and 13 are reserved for the two goalkeepers.

If a player's cap comes off, it should be replaced at an appropriate break in play, typically after a goal, or between quarters. This is an example of how referees will try their best to keep the game going, and only stop it if essential.

Water polo balls are generally yellow and of varying size and weight for juniors, women and men.

Chapter Three: Officials and Players

Officials and Time Clocks

As water polo is a fast flowing, and high scoring game, it is hard for one referee to keep up with play. So ideally there should be two referees, two goal judges, one secretary and one timekeeper. The secretary and timekeeper sit on a scoring table on one side of the pool. Each team has a bench, where the coach, team officials and substitutes sit, on the opposite side to the table.

One referee with a timekeeper and secretary is the minimum to run a game. The secretary records: (1) the goals, and who scored them; and (2) exclusion fouls – and alerts the referee when a player has reached the maximum (three) and can no longer play in the game. All this information, and the times at which they occurred, are written on a score sheet as shown in Figure 8.

The timekeeper runs two clocks. One indicates the time remaining in the quarter; and the other (called the shot clock) is needed as the offensive team only has possession of the ball for 30 seconds without shooting for a goal.

Every time a referee blows their whistle in open play both clocks are stopped.

Running two clocks is harder than it seems, especially as both have to be stopped when there is a break in play indicted by the referee's whistle - then

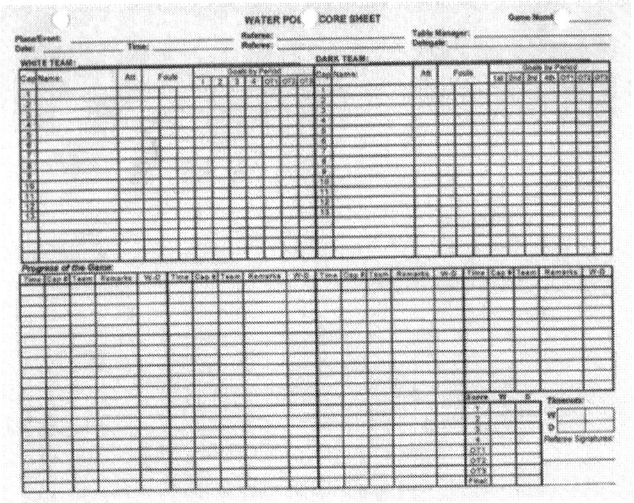

Figure 8. Water polo score sheet

both restarted as play resumes. Also, as the referee does not whistle when free, goal, corner and neutral throws are to be taken, the timekeeper has to keep a close eye of the game (to restart both clocks), as well as listen to the referee's whistle.

As in basketball, the shot clock in water polo is designed to speed up the game. Other rules also help to speed up the game: the need to take throws (foul, goal or corner) without delay; the advantage rule; fouls (ordinary and exclusion) against a defender for 'pinning down' an attacker in possession of the ball; and fouls can also be given for time wasting. Also, a penalty is given if a coach (or other team official) delays the game.

The shot clock indicates how much time remains for the offensive team to shoot the ball. But if a shot is taken and the ball rebounds, the shot clock is reset and the 30 seconds begins again. So hitting the goalpost is not a bad thing if possession is retained, as the attacking team have another 30 seconds to score a goal.[14]

---

[14] Note 2019 FINA rule change: Clock resets. The timekeeper will

The shot clock is also reset if there is an exclusion foul or corner, but not an ordinary foul (see later). At all other stoppages of play – eg a free throw (after an ordinary foul), or goal, neutral or penalty throw – the clock is stopped but not reset. The ball is put back in play (and clock restarted) when the ball leaves the hand of the player taking the appropriate throw, or when touched by a player following a neutral throw.

The shot clock leads to high scoring games in sports like water polo and basketball. Other sports like football (soccer), for example, do not have one. This is part of the reason why, in such sports, few goals may be scored. Whereas it's not unusual in water polo, for teams to score over 10 goals.

The timekeeper whistles (or indicates by some method), when the 30 second shot clock is up, when there is 15 seconds left on a one minute timeout, and when there is one minute left in the match. Regarding the timeout, it is conventional that the timekeeper blows three short whistles at 15 seconds to go, then the referee passes the ball to the goalkeeper (usually) on halfway, with the referee blowing a long whistle to restart play. The referee should pause and wait for both teams to get into position, before the whistle is blown.

Referees

Regarding refereeing in general, it is important in water polo to 'respect the whistle' at all times. This is true for players, coaches, supporting staff, and spectators. Ie, the referee's decision is final. The referees have ultimate power over decisions relating to the game, even (if necessary) over-ruling decisions from goal judges, secretary or timekeeper.

The referees also have the power to abandon the game at any time during a match. Only the captain

---

reset the clock to 20 seconds when a. the ball is put into play after awarding a corner throw, b. after a rebound after a shot which does not cause change of possession, and c. after an exclusion foul.

can (politely) question the referee, at the appropriate time (eg between quarters). All need to accept that referees will make mistakes, and this is part of sport.

At a practical level, there has to be a way in which the two referees 'divide up the field'. This is usually done by each drawing an imaginary diagonal line across the pool, with the short side of the triangle to the referee's right. The referee then supervises the triangle on their side of the pool, reserving the right to make decisions about events on the other referee's domain, especially if they have missed something.

The 'lead referee' is the one on the side of the scoring table. He/she starts the game, and restarts it at the start of each quarter.

The referee will acknowledge a goal on their side of the pool, and lead the restart (ie whistle) after a goal on their side.

Can you talk to the referee(s)? Yes, please do. But it should be after the game is over and the referee(s) have signed the score sheet. It is best done after you have changed, ie when the hurly-burly of the game has settled down. They may then answer questions. It is best to assume a conversational non-challenging tone, eg "could you explain to me why that decision was made at the end of the 2nd quarter?" etc.

Referee's Whistles

With all the splashing and shouting in the pool, it is hard to hear what is going on in the general melee of the game. Because of this noise, referees use a combination of the whistle and a special water polo sign language. The signals that make up this language are described in chapter seven.

So, it is very important for both offensive and defensive teams to listen for the referee's whistle (and the referee to whistle loudly). Why? The whistle guides the players in the direction of play, and other issues.

In the modern age, many referees just use a short

and a long whistle. But, traditionally, referees use three types of whistle to help further:

- One (short) whistle: defensive ordinary foul (offence keeps the ball);
- Two (short) whistles: offensive ordinary foul (defence gets the ball, ie possession changes);
- Three whistles (two short and one long): exclusion/penalty fouls (offence keeps the ball).

There is variation concerning whistles, and not all referees will follow these patterns.

Also, when an exclusion foul occurs, it is important for the offensive team to identify where the excluded player is (or was) in the pool – ie where the defensive player is missing from. For the attack it is a good idea to attack there; and for the defence, to fill the gap. More about that later.

Players

The role of outfield players change constantly from offence to defence and vice versa in water polo. In other words, offensive players hold defensive positions as well. For instance, the point (typically involved in the offence), may become the centre back when defending. Figure 7 in the previous chapter shows the basic offensive positions.

Every single player including the goalkeeper should play offence. Players that fail to actively take part in the offence expose their team to pressure, as the defence will leave a player that is not a threat in order to help their team-mates. Similarly, every single player should play defence. Failing to take part, will expose your team-mates to more players than they are able to guard.

The best offence is good defence. As each period in water polo lasts eight minutes, a split-second lapse in defence could gift your opponent a goal.

Centre Forward

The centre forward (or 'centre', 'hole set' or 'pit man') is one of the most important positions in the game, as they are located nearest to the opponents' goal. This player is usually on or near the two metre line, in front of the goal, and is normally the player who takes most shots. Balls are usually passed to the centre forward using a 'wet pass' (on the water, rather than hand-to-hand, ie a 'dry pass'); after which the centre forward may attempt to shoot, or try to draw an exclusion foul from a defender.

The centre forward position is a specialised position that requires a different set of skills compared to the other outfield players. It is useful to have more than one (three or more is good) who can play centre forward, so the 'main centre forward' player gets short 'rests'. Also, if there is only one centre forward, the defending team, will know exactly who to focus on in every attack, which makes it easier for them to mark him/her out of the game.

Driver (or Flat)

This position of driver is played by two of the five perimeter players. The drivers lead the offence, along with the centre forward (and point). Drivers are constantly creating movement by driving down to the goal post and rotating around; or creating screens, in order to free team-mates off their defenders. Their main job is to get the ball to the centre forward. Their proximity to the goal and their position relative to the centre forward, puts them in a good position for scoring goals. They also need to be aware of not playing too near the centre forward and getting in their way.

Drivers should also be fast swimmers as they swim the most, moving from defence to offence and vice versa, all the time.

Wings

Wings play on either side of the goal near the 2 metre line. The offensive wings' aim is to 'set the ball', get themselves open to receive passes, pass the ball to the centre forward, and take some shots themselves (if the angle is good enough). Due to their proximity to goal, the defensive wings are in the perfect position to recover rebounds (a failed shot, leading to an unguarded ball in the water) and launch an offensive attempt against the other team.

The offensive wings may also 'set a screen' for the driver and other team-mates who are receiving or in possession of the ball. This means to intentionally delay (or block) the opposing defender so as to allow his team-mate to swim by.

Point
The point is furthest away from the middle of the goal. This player often directs attacking play and is a good long-distance shooter. This player is often the one who facilitates most of the passes and throws – like the flyhalf in rugby union, or quarterback in American football – in order to move the ball across the pool and towards his team-mates. The position of point makes it easy for them to communicate to their team-mates and hence organise the offensive strategy.

Both wet and dry passes should be used by the point as they are in a central position, but wet passes should be used when a team-mate is being closely guarded by an opposing defender.

The point may become the centre back (see below) on defence. This is partly so they will have less distance to swim to get to the centre back position, ideally before the centre forward gets there.

Defence
There are only two players with fixed defensive positions, while other players defend in general and do not have specific positions.

Goalkeeper
The goalkeeper is vital to the outcome of the game. The person playing this position has a vital defensive role whilst also supporting their team-mates in

attack. Goalkeepers must always be aware of their position in the goal, relative to the ball in play. A goalkeeper has to focus on the ball at all times, to make sure they are ready if a player decides to shoot.

It is important for a goalkeeper to jump high in the water in order to block any high incoming shots. But low shots also occur, especially the low 'skip-shot'. This is when the ball is bounced on the surface of the water and into the goal. Hence it is important for the goalkeeper to cover low shots as well.

It is also important for goalkeepers to stay engaged in the game as a whole. They have a complete view of the pool, in both attack and defence. So they are able to see things happening other players might miss. With that knowledge, they play an important role in communicating what they see to their team-mates, continuously talking (often shouting) that knowledge to them.

For example, in defence, they are responsible for calling defensive plays, positioning of blockers, and the strength of the opponent's' offence. In attack, they are responsible for communicating which players are in good position to receive the ball, time remaining on the shot clock, and any weakness in the opponent's defence.

Goalkeeper Rules
There are special rules for goalkeepers, as in many sports. Unlike the rest of the players, a goalkeeper is allowed to walk or stand on the bottom of the pool. He/she can hit the ball with their fist, and can touch or catch the ball with both hands. These privileges only exist within 6 metres. Outside that 'normal field player rules' apply to the goalkeeper. A goalkeeper can score a goal but must not go past halfway.[15] So, unlike in football (soccer), a goalkeeper cannot 'go forward' for a corner, say, at the end of the game.

---

[15] Note 2019 FINA rule change: Goalkeeper. The goalkeeper is allowed to be anywhere in the pool; ie they can move beyond halfway and touch the ball; and so they can also take a penalty, if required.

The goalkeeper (or defender) is not allowed to move the net during play (say to block a goal) or sink the ball within 6 metres. If they (or a defender) does so, a penalty is awarded to the other team.

Centre Back

The centre back (or 'Hole-D', ie hole defence) position exists only during defensive play. Their role is to defend against the centre forward in front of the goal, usually on the 2 metre line. The centre back is the only player besides the goalkeeper to have most access to the goal, and is therefore normally the second-to-last line of defence.

The centre back will position themselves on the centre forward, based on the type of defence the team is playing. This means they could be behind, in front of, or on the side of the centre forward. Once the ball is passed to the centre forward, the centre back will try to prevent the centre forward from scoring, including stealing the ball. Again, being a key defensive role focussing on the centre forward, it is a specialised position.

If the centre back plays on the side of a (right-handed) centre forward, one technique is for the centre back to rest their chin on left shoulder of the centre forward, with the left arm in front the centre forward's head, obscuring their view, and the right hand on the back of the elbow, to block a backhand shot.

The centre back may become the point when possession changes and his/her team goes on the offensive.

General

Players have to be sure to defend against the drivers of the opposing team, as these players are normally the fastest swimmers and are responsible for passing to the centre forward or shooting on goal themselves. Another player to defend against is the centre forward, who is most likely to score goals during a match. This is why the centre forward has a specific defender against him/her, ie the centre back.

There is another very important principle of defence: in water polo, you do not need the ball. You will definitely get the ball back, either after a goal or when the 30 second shot clock expires. So the main aim of defence is to slow down the offence, and limit their shooting opportunities. It is not necessary to aggressively try to steal the ball all of the time.

Body Types
Certain body types are more suited for particular positions, eg the centre forward will tend to be a stronger, larger player. Left-handed players are especially coveted on the right-hand side of the field; allowing teams to launch two-sided attacks.

Positional Set-up

The most common positional set-up is known as the 'arc' (as shown in Figure 7 in Chapter Two). These are numbered '1' to '5' counting from the right of the arc (or left to right in the USA). Player '6' is the centre-forward, who is usually on the 2 metre line, in front of the goal. Other options (often used in a 'man-up' situation; see later) for an offensive set-up are: (1) a '3–3', so called because there are two lines in front of the opponent's goal; or (2) a '4–2', where there are two centre forwards in front of the goal, two wings, and two in the backline.

Chapter Four:
Starting Play and Throws

Rules of Water Polo

Even though water polo is a simple game, there are quite a lot of rules. This is because it a fast contact sport so tempers can get frayed easily. The rules enable the referee(s) to carry out their two basic tasks: a. keep the speed of the game up and maximise goals; and b. control the game, and thereby protect the players, and stop them getting hurt. Thus few serious injuries happen in water polo.

Regarding the former task, referees may use their discretion to apply the rules 'harder' or 'softer' according to the type of match and players' experience. This is the art rather than science of refereeing.

It is important for referees to remember that the game is primarily for the players (and those watching them); their role is to help them enjoy it within the framework of the rules.

This is the first of three chapters that focus on the rules.

Before the Game

The referee(s) will greet the two captains, then toss a coin to see who starts at which end. If it is an all deep water pool, there may not be a toss. Then, by convention, the home team will start from the left of the scoring table (ie on the referee's left with their back to the table), and away team will start from the right.

Some pools are not long enough to have a re-entry area. So the referee(s) will explain the local rules re exclusions. This is usually for the excluded player to get out of the pool and sit on the edge, with feet out of the pool.

They will check the nails of the players (to prevent scratching in the game). After that, when the players are ready, they will blow the whistle and start the game.

Starting Play

The start of each period is very exciting. Players take up positions on their respective goal lines at the start of each period; one metre apart and no closer than one metre from the goal posts. The lead referee (on the side of the scoring table) whistles and drops the ball on to the water; and both teams then swim to the midpoint of the pool (this is known as the 'sprint' or 'swim-off'). The clock starts when the first player touches the ball.

Restarting Play (after a goal is scored)

After a goal is scored, the teams may line up anywhere within their own half of the pool. In practice, this is usually near the centre of the pool. They go on the offensive as soon as the referee whistles to start the action; and the team not scoring the goal, puts the ball in to play by passing it backwards to a team mate.

At a start or restart, the player taking it cannot score directly. Another player (of either team, but not the defending goalkeeper) must intentionally touch the ball, before a goal can be scored, ie they can pass to another player who can shoot and score. This is similar to the rule for free throws after ordinary fouls (see later).

Playing Area

The playing area ('pitch') is that area between the goal line, and the sides of the pool. If the ball goes outside this area (or hits the side of the pool before hitting the water, and rebounds back into the pool), the referee blows the whistle to stop the game – and awards the relevant throw. This will be a free throw, if the ball goes out of the side of the pool (taken at the point where the ball left the pool); or a goal or corner throw, if the ball goes behind the goal. The whistle also tells the timekeeper to stop the clock(s).

The ball can touch the side of the pool and stay in play.

If, in a break in play, the ball is on the water at the edge of the pool, the referee should not 'try to be helpful' and pick the ball up – as returning it may lead to an advantage to one team.

Goal, Corner and Free Throws

All have to be taken without delay. As well as the shot clock, this helps to speed up the game. You are allowed about three seconds[16] to play the ball. Thus time is not given to 'organise a play' in water polo. If delay occurs, the throw is reversed.

An opponent should back off to about 1.5–2 metres[17] from the throw taker, and cannot interfere with the taking of the throw – eg if a player throws the ball in the air or places it on the water, the opposing player cannot try and take the ball off the player. Also the defender cannot 'hold their ground' (ie stay where

---

[16] This is actually not defined in the rules. But 3 seconds is roughly when most referees would apply the 'undue delay' rule.

[17] Again, not defined in the rules. But 1.5–2 metres is a reasonable distance apart.

they are); they have to make an active movement away from the attacker to give them space to play. Not doing so (or interfering in other ways) is quite heavily penalised, with an exclusion foul.

The 'throw' can be a pass to another player, or the ball can be dribbled out. As dribbling the ball out is allowed, not being able to pass to a team-mate, is not a reason for delaying the throw.

The referee will whistle (short blast) to indicate a break in play for a goal, corner or free flow. No whistle is then needed for the attacking team to take the throw.

As in football (soccer), there is an 'Advantage Rule' in water polo (FINA Rule 7.3) – ie the referee has the discretion to award (or not award) any ordinary, exclusion or penalty foul; depending on whether the decision would advantage the attacking team. So referees do their best to keep the game flowing; and will often choose to ignore fouls committed away from the action, so as not to prevent scoring opportunities.

Goal Throw

A goal throw is awarded to the defending team, when *any* player (other than the goalkeeper of the defending team) of *either* team causes the ball to pass beyond the goal line. In this way the rule is different from the goal kick in football (soccer). It can be taken by any player (usually the nearest) of the defending team, from anywhere within the 2 metre area.

The is no referee arm action to indicate a goal throw in the rules. But the referee will whistle (short blast) to indicate a goal throw, and point away from the goal. It is then taken without another whistle. It must be taken without delay. If not, the referee will whistle again, and award a free throw to the opposite team.

Corner Throw

A corner throw is awarded when the goalkeeper touches the ball from a shot at goal and the ball passes beyond the goal line, or when a defending player deliberately sends the ball over the goal line. So, again, this rule is unlike football (soccer) when defenders often concede corners. The corner throw is taken from the 2 metre mark, on the side nearest to which the ball crossed the goal line. Any player of the attacking team (usually the nearest) can take the throw.[18]

There is no referee arm action to indicate a corner throw in the rules. But the referee will whistle (short blast) to indicate a corner throw, and point towards the goal (ie opposite from a goal throw). Then the referee will indicate which side of the pool on the 2 metre line, they want it taken from. They may hold up two fingers (to indicate the 2 metre line). It is then taken without another whistle. It must be taken without delay. If not, the referee will whistle again, and award a free throw to the opposite team.

Free Throw

A free throw is awarded to a team when an opponent commits an ordinary or exclusion foul; or if the ball leaves the side of the pool; or if a ball hits the edge of the pool 'on the full' (ie without touching the water first) and rebounds back.

The player who takes a free throw may (without delay) either: pass the ball to a team-mate; drop it in front of him/herself and play it (ie dribble); or shoot at goal if the foul occurred outside 6 metres. If a player takes a shot at goal (for a foul outside 6 metres), the shot must be taken in one motion, ie immediately as they take the throw.

---

[18] Note 2019 FINA rule change: Corner throw. A player taking a corner throw can: a. shoot directly, b. swim and shoot without passing, or c. pass to another player.

After an ordinary foul, the player taking the free throw cannot score directly (unless outside 6 metres, taken immediately with one action). Another player (of either team) must intentionally touch the ball, before a goal can be scored, ie they can pass to another player who can shoot and score.[19] This is not necessary for a free throw after an exclusion foul, eg the taker of the throw can dribble a bit, then score.

Furthermore, dribbling means dribbling. In other words, on taking the throw, you cannot 'steal a metre' by moving 1–2 metres forward to get nearer to the goal. Also you cannot push off the defender to get more space, or stop them putting their arm up for example.

The free throw is taken from the point where the foul occurred, or behind it;[20] or on the 2 metre line, if the foul takes place within the other team's 2 metre zone.[21] It is usually taken by the player on whom the foul was committed, but can be taken by any player (including the goalkeeper, if the foul occurred in their half).

The referee indicates a free throw by a short blast of the whistle and pointing with one arm in the direction of the attack. It is then taken without another whistle. It must be taken without delay. If not, the referee will whistle again, and award a free throw to the opposite team.

If a referee awards a free throw the 'wrong' way, he/she should whistle again; if there are two referees, their arms may point in opposite directions. The nearest referee that has whistled should then ask for the ball by showing rotating cupped hands. This gives that referee time to think; and, if necessary, consult the other referee.

---

[19] Note 2019 FINA rule change: Free throw after ordinary foul outside 6 metres. The taker of the throw can score without the ball touching another player.

[20] There is an exception. If the ball is further from the defending team's goal, it can be taken from the location of the ball.

[21] Note 2019 FINA rule change: Free throw. A free throw shall be taken from the location of the ball.

Then, when the decision is made, both teams should be allowed a few seconds to adjust their positions. The ball is given to the nearest player of the correct team, and the free throw is taken the right way. If a referee states they have made a mistake, and the foul is reversed, this may help to keep the peace.

Neutral Throw

A neutral throw is awarded when the referee cannot be 100% sure who committed the first foul, if two fouls appear to occur simultaneously – such as when two players take the ball under the water. Also if two referees make opposing decisions at the same time, and neither are sure, one may restart with a neutral throw.

The referee stops the game with a short blast of the whistle, and indicates a neutral throw with both thumbs up, and asks for the ball with rotating cupped hands. He/she whistles (to restart the clocks), and puts the ball back in play, with each team given an equal chance to get it. The ball can be touched before it reaches the water. But the two players cannot move

Figure 9. Penalty Throw

before the referee's whistle; or push off the other player or the bottom of the pool.

Penalty Throw

A penalty throw is awarded to a team when an opponent commits a penalty foul in the 6 metre area.[22] Any player (except the goalkeeper) can take the penalty throw (which is taken on the 5 metre line); they must throw the ball at the goal without delay (and without faking the throw) when the whistle is blown.

The penalty taker's body cannot cross the 5 metre line until after the ball is released. All players except the defending goalkeeper must be outside the 5 metre area. The goalkeeper must not be in front of the goal line. One defender can be 2 metres either side of the penalty taker. Figure 9 shows a penalty throw being taken.

If the ball rebounds from the goal post, crossbar or goalkeeper, it remains in play, ie an attacker can quickly 'tip the ball' into the goal. So it is important for both teams to keep playing after a penalty is taken, in case a goal is not scored and the ball stays in play.

---

[22] Note 2019 FINA rule change: Penalty. Inside 6 metres, when a player is swimming with, and/or holding the ball, and is impeded (attacked) from behind during an attempt to shoot, a penalty foul must be awarded.

Chapter Five: Ordinary and Exclusion Fouls

There are three kinds of foul: ordinary, exclusion and penalty fouls. Exclusion fouls have three types: simple (described in this chapter), misconduct and brutality.

The commonest foul is the ordinary foul. Most players will have one or more awarded against them during a game. There is no upper limit of ordinary fouls. The clock is stopped (but not reset) after an ordinary foul.

The (simple) exclusion foul is the next commonest. It is more commonly called just an 'Exclusion' or 'Major' Foul. Most exclusion fouls are simple ones, and result in the player being excluded for 20 seconds with return allowed. Players are only allowed three such exclusion fouls. Any more and they are excluded from the game.[23] The offending player usually remains on the bench traditionally with their cap strings undone. The clock is stopped and reset (for another 30 seconds) after an exclusion foul (and a corner). This increases the 'value' of an exclusion foul (or corner).

These two types of foul are an intrinsic part of the sport of water polo; as it is a skill to draw fouls, and not to concede them (or at least to only concede the

---

[23] Ironically at the end of the season there is an 'anti-hero' status to the player who is top of a league table known as 'Major Kings' (ie those who were most frequently excluded after three exclusion fouls).

lesser ordinary foul). They will therefore be described in some detail.

The other two (higher level) exclusion fouls lead to the exclusion of the player for the entire game; either with a substitute allowed back after 20 seconds (Misconduct foul, or 'wrapped'); or with a substitute allowed back after four minutes (Brutality foul). Both of these are equivalent to a red card in football (soccer) or rugby union. Some fouls lead to a penalty throw awarded to the opposing team (Penalty foul). These latter three fouls are covered in the next chapter.

Ordinary Foul

= Free throw awarded to fouled team

The most common ordinary foul is impeding the free movement of a player who is *in possession of but NOT holding the ball* (this is how FINA rule 20.9 (= not to "push or push off an opponent who is not holding the ball") is interpreted); and not strong enough to receive an exclusion foul. Figure 10 (below) shows physical play. But it is a fair challenge and not an ordinary (or exclusion, see later) foul as the defender is holding the ball. Whereas Figure 11 (below) shows an ordinary foul, as the offensive player is not holding the ball;

Figure 10. A fair challenge. Not an ordinary (or exclusion) foul (offensive player holding the ball)

Figure 11. An ordinary foul
(offensive player not holding the ball)

Most of these are given to the attacker (referees will favour the attacker), if the defender is 'too physical' (but not enough to gain an exclusion foul). The most common foul is when a player reaches over the shoulder of an opponent in order to knock the ball away and thereby hinders the opponent. Offensive players can receive ordinary fouls as well; for example, if they push off a defender to provide space for a pass or shot.

But, strangely, there is no rule that states this explicitly – FINA 20.9 is the nearest to it. And, unlike many sports, ordinary fouls are not always bad. Nonetheless, they are both a standard defensive and offensive tactic and cause the majority of free throws. They are accepted part of the game.

They can be used as a defensive tactic to slow down the attack (which allows the other defenders to get back in position, and so prevent scoring). Alternatively, offensive players will sometimes attempt to 'draw' a foul (by releasing the ball, and encouraging the defender to foul them); to earn a free (and better) pass, and allow team-mates to move forward. Thus it is not uncommon for more offensive movement immediately after an ordinary foul has been called. An offensive foul can be also be used to maximise scoring, by allowing the attacker to shoot on goal (if they are outside 6 metres).

The skill (for the defender) is to slow down the game in this way without being over-aggressive and giving away an exclusion foul. The skill (for the attacker) is to 'draw the foul' by briefly letting go the ball, so the defender's badgering of them turns into an ordinary foul – and they are awarded a free throw. Why? With a defender badgering them a good throw is (and should be) difficult.

When an attacker looks at the referee to question why a foul is not being given against them, the referee may make a hand sign like a cup (indicating you are still holding the ball); so if you want a foul (under FINA 20.9), you have to let go of it (and risk losing it of course).

An ordinary foul is also awarded against a player by the referee if they commit any of these offences:

- Advance beyond the goal line before the start or restart of game;
- Assist a player at the start or restart of game (eg a 'sling-shot');
- Push off the posts or sides or back of the pool;

NB: these three fouls often occur at the start of play in each quarter; the non-offending team then receives a free throw from the halfway line;

- Walk on[24] or push off the bottom of the pool. This may be seen as a jump in the shallow end; by an offensive player shooting, or a defensive player blocking. This rule does not apply to the goal-keeper inside the 6 metre line;
- Hold the ball under water (also called 'ball under');[25] ie in water polo, one cannot hide the ball

---

[24] Tired players may walk when they get to the shallow end. If not interfering with play, referees may not impose this rule too strongly.

[25] The referee should be able to see the ball at all times. If they

under the water. The attacking person in possession commits the foul if this happens, even if the defender pushes the attacker's hand down. It makes no difference if it against the player's will;

- But if a goalkeeper (or other defending player) takes the ball under the water within 6 metres, a penalty is awarded (see next chapter);
- Hit the ball with a clenched fist; again, if a defending player (other than the goalkeeper) plays the ball with a clenched fist within 6 metres, a penalty is awarded (see next chapter);
- Touch the ball with both hands at the same time; again, if a defending player (other than the goalkeeper) attempts to block a shot (or pass) with two hands within 6 metres, a penalty is awarded (see next chapter);
- Push, or push off from, an opponent *not* holding the ball (impeding); this is the only rule (FINA 20.9) that alludes to most of the fouls against a defender that are an intrinsic part of the sport of water polo. It is also used against an attacker, eg pushing off the defender with the arm (or leg) to gain space to pass or shoot;
- To be within 2 metres of the goal without the ball (you can swim into 2 metres with the ball[26]); this is often overlooked if the attacker is well to the side of the pool especially when the ball is on the other side of the pool;
- Take a penalty throw incorrectly; and the penalty is reversed, and becomes a free throw to the defending team;
- Delay taking a free, goal or corner throw; then the throw is reversed;
- If the goalkeeper goes past the centre line;
- Tip the ball out of the field of play. This will lead to a free throw (to the opposition) if the ball goes

---

cannot, it must be 'ball under'. Deciding who the culprit is, is not always that easy.

[26] If the receiver of the ball is on or behind the 2 metre line as the ball is released, and swims into 2 metres, this is allowed.

off the side of the pool; or a goal throw if over the goal line (or corner throw if the referee thinks the player has done it deliberately);

- Deliberately waste time. One example is when the goalkeeper starts play, after say catching a shot. The goalkeeper has (theoretically) got 30 seconds of the shot clock to play the ball. But they must show intent to pass the ball, not just hold on to it, and have a think about where to pass. Also, if there is an intent (by a player, coach or any team official) to prevent a probable goal or delay the game, this can also lead to a penalty being awarded (see later);

- Simulate being fouled;[27] along with the previous indication for an ordinary foul, the referee can use this rule to make the sure the game moves on swiftly and legally.

If the centre back and centre forward are wrestling for position without a serious attempt to harm one another (and not interfering with play), most referees will let that happen, and award no ordinary foul. So ordinary fouls are rare in the pit.

The referee signals an ordinary foul with a whistle,[28] and holding one arm out straight in the direction of the attack. He/she may also point to where they want the throw taken from. After an ordinary foul, the nearest member of the fouled team (usually the player on whom the foul was committed) puts the ball into play by taking a free throw. This can be a pass to another player, or the ball can be dribbled out, or a shot can be taken at goal (if taken immediately in one action) if the ordinary foul occurs outside 6 metres.

---

[27] A yellow card can also be given to a player who shows very obvious (or repeated) simulation. This is not common. It may be given with or without a previous ordinary foul (ie a warning).

[28] Traditionally a referee will give one short blast if the foul is given to the attacking player (in possession of the ball); and two short blasts if the foul is against the attacker with the ball, and possession reverses (to the defending team).

Exclusion Foul – Simple

= Exclusion (and return, or substitution) for 20 seconds, and free throw to fouled team

(Simple) exclusion fouls are called for more serious offences. They are commonly awarded against a defender for impeding an attacker, in a more aggressive way than that seen in an ordinary foul (see earlier). Such fouls occur, for example, when the defensive player 'holds, sinks or pulls back' (a key phrase in the rules) the offensive player *in possession of but NOT holding the ball* – especially if the defender attacks the neck or head of the attacker. Figure 12 shows such an exclusion foul, as the player behind is pulling his opponent back by the neck, and the opponent is not holding the ball.

Figure 12: Exclusion foul

In the next example (Figure 13), the player with the blue cap is attacking the face of the player in the white cap, who is not holding the ball.

Figure 13: Another exclusion foul

Again, strangely (as it is probably the commonest cause of an exclusion foul), there is also not really a rule to back up many of these fouls. Rules FINA 21.8 (not allowing a player to "impede or otherwise prevent free movement of a player who is not holding the ball") and 21.9 ("hold, sink or pull back an opponent who is not holding the ball") are used to validate such decisions – in a similar way to rule 20.9 for ordinary fouls. An exclusion foul is then assigned to the player who commits it. Thus, an exclusion foul is often referred to as a 'personal foul'. And a free throw is awarded the other team.

The player is sent out of the pool, for 20 seconds, leaving his team one person down ('man-down'). The excluded player should move to their re-entry area, without delay and without leaving the water. The 20 second exclusion period starts when the free throw is taken. If they delay or interfere with play, they receive another personal foul, and a penalty is awarded.

If the other team scores a goal while he/she is off, or possession changes, he/she can return to the game immediately. Otherwise the re-entry of the excluded player is signalled on expiration of 20 seconds by the referee indicating they can re-enter the playing area, or by a table official by holding up flags (blue or white, as cap colour indicates).

An exclusion foul is also awarded against a player by the referee if they commit any of these offences:

- Sit on steps or side of pool;
- Splash an opponent in the face;
- Interfere with a free, goal or corner throw;
- Block a pass or shot with two hands, inside 5 metres; if the referee thinks that this action would have prevented a goal, a penalty can be awarded (see later);
- Use two hands to hold an opponent who is not holding the ball. But one hand can be placed on an opponent without the ball. This is often done partly so the holder knows where the opponent is;
- *Impede* (ie prevent free movement) a player who is

not holding the ball (excludes dribbling). This includes swimming across the legs or back of an opponent to slow them down;

- *Hold, sink or pull back* (a useful summary phrase to describe most exclusion fouls) an opponent who is *not* holding the ball (excludes dribbling). If sinking is due to a player going over the head of another player, this is always an exclusion foul;
- Kick or strike an opponent (or show an intent to); if this occurs within 6 metres, a penalty throw is also awarded. The referee can decide to punish a kick or strike in this way, or with a Misconduct or Brutality foul (see later) depending on intent, and effect;
- For an excluded player to interfere with play, or not leave immediately. Another exclusion (personal) foul is recorded on that player, and a penalty is awarded. This action is thus heavily sanctioned in water polo;
- For an excluded player to re-enter (or substitute to enter) improperly; eg, without a signal from the referee (or scoring table), or not from the re-entry area, or by lifting the rope. They are excluded (again) but only one personal foul is recorded. And a penalty is awarded (if the player's team is not in possession of the ball);[29]
- For the defending goalkeeper to fail to take up the correct position at the taking of a penalty throw, having been ordered once to do so by the referee.

The 'hold, sink or pull back' indication is not enforced strongly on the centre forward and centre back. In other words, if their wrestling is not interfering with play outside the pit, and is not obviously dangerous, they are largely left to 'get on with it'. When called, it is usually against the centre back for being over-aggressive just after the ball has come in. This is the commonest reason for an exclusion foul.

---

[29] If the offence is committed by a player of the team in possession of the ball, they are excluded again and a free throw is awarded to the opposing team.

This makes the defending team 'man-down' and a goal more likely. Ordinary fouls are not often given in this situation.

The referee signals an exclusion foul in this manner: (1) three blasts of the whistle (two short, one long); (2) pointing at the excluded player then moving the arm towards their re-entry area; then (3) putting up one or both hands and signalling the number of the excluded player.

As well as the referee excluding the player, a free throw is awarded to the other team. As with ordinary fouls, this should be taken without delay. If not, the decision is reversed.

The referee may award a 'double exclusion foul', ie to two players at once (usually when they are competing against each other, with or without the ball). These are more often given for incidents in the main field of play off the ball (rather than in the pit).

To indicate a double exclusion foul, the referee should whistle loudly, ask for (and hold) the ball to calm things down, then send both players out; and inform the table of what is happening and which players are excluded. Then, when everyone in the pool is set up and ready – and know exactly what is happening – the referee should give the ball to the team that were attacking before the double exclusion decision. The free throw should then be taken without delay. If neither team was clearly attacking, a neutral throw should be given at the point where the foul(s) occurred.

In such double exclusion fouls, the shot-clock is stopped but not reset, as for a single exclusion foul.

Chapter Six: Other Exclusion and Penalty Fouls

This chapter covers more serious fouls. This includes Misconduct and Brutality exclusion fouls (both uncommon), and Penalty fouls.

Exclusion Foul – Misconduct ('Wrapped')

= sent off for rest of game, leave pool area, red card, with substitution at 20 seconds

A misconduct exclusion foul (with substitution at 20 seconds) is reserved for serious infractions, usually unsportsman-like behaviour. Generally, this kind of foul is given either for violence or disrespect. As a result of this foul, the offending player is removed from the game (and has to leave the pool area). Misconduct offences are of two types:

With no penalty awarded:

- The use of unacceptable language (eg swearing[30] to the referee or anyone else) should be punished severely. The rules do not distinguish between swearing at yourself (maybe in frustration for a

---

[30] What about minor comments to the referee (eg, "why didn't you call a foul?") or minor taunting of other players? They are not specifically banned in the rules. But many referees will punish the first one with an exclusion foul; then after that with a Misconduct foul (ie sent off for the rest of the game).

mistake) or at someone; so technically both should receive a Misconduct foul;

- At a junior level, swearing at oneself is sometimes punished with an exclusion foul (and maybe a verbal warning); whereas at senior level, this too leads to a Misconduct foul. Of course there is an argument for the response to be the same at both levels; so a junior player does not become a senior player that swears;
- Aggressive or persistent foul play;
- Refusing obedience to, or showing disrespect to a referee or official (eg back-chat to referee);
- Behaviour against the spirit of the rules and likely to bring the game into disrepute. For example, this rule can be used to sanction recurrent foul simulation. This rule can also be used against a coach, a player on the bench, other official or spectator. A yellow card may be given first, as a last warning;
- Interfering with the taking of a penalty throw. Then the penalty will taken (or re-taken) as necessary.

With penalty awarded – ie these two offences are heavily sanctioned in water polo:

- For a player (or substitute) who is not entitled to participate in the play at that time to enter the field of play; for example, if a player (or substitute) with three exclusions re-enters the pool. He/she is sent off for Misconduct and a penalty is awarded. Or, if a team has more players in the pool than they are allowed, at any time during play, a penalty is given to the opposing team;
- For the goalkeeper (or any defending player) to pull over the goal completely, with the object of preventing a probable goal. He/she is sent off for Misconduct and a penalty is awarded.

The referee signals a misconduct exclusion foul in this manner: (1) a long blast of the whistle; (2) he/she makes a circular motion with both hands (a la 'Saturday Night Fever', with the foul often called being 'wrapped'); (3) then putting up one or both hands, indicating the number of the excluded player(s); and, (4) a red card is shown.

Exclusion Foul – Brutality

= sent off for rest of game, leave pool area, red card, with substitution at 4 minutes and Penalty Throw

If a player deliberately strikes – or attempts to strike – another player, using any part of the body, the player will be excluded from the game (Brutality[31]). It can also be given for offensive language or arguing with the referee. A substitute player can enter the field of play after 4 minutes of play.

This is a very serious offence. The brutality foul requires that the offending player demonstrates obvious intent to injure another player. This is much more serious than mere aggression.

As a result of this foul, the offending player is removed from the game (and has to leave the pool area) and excluded for (at least) the next game. And the offended team is awarded a penalty throw.

The referee signals a brutality exclusion foul in this manner: (1) a long blast of the whistle; (2) low arms crossed with fists; (3) then putting up one or both hands, indicating the number of the excluded player(s); and, (4) a red card is shown.

What constitutes brutality foul is, to a degree, subjective. All referees will agree that a punch, kick or elbow with intent to injure warrants a brutality foul. But what is the difference between a. reaching for (or around) the neck or head of an opponent (which usually leads to an exclusion foul); and b. doing this with such a force that it is, in effect, a blow? An obser-

---

[31] Brutality fouls occur very rarely. If a player is excluded for brutality, the rest of the team will not be happy or impressed, as being 'man-down' for 4 minutes is a long time and several goals are likely to be scored. Also being told to leave the pool is embarrassing and the player is unlikely to want that to happen again.

vant referee will try to spot such behaviour and issue a brutality foul.

All brutality fouls have to be reported by officials to the relevant governing body.

Penalty Foul

Penalty fouls may be awarded on their own, or in association with a Misconduct foul; the former being more common.

A penalty foul is usually given for foul play within 6 metres. Most are given against a defending player who fouls an attacking player in such a way that prevents them from scoring, when they would have had a good chance to do so. Furthermore, the attacking player's head and upper body have to face goal, and they must show a clear intent to score.

Penalty Foul alone (without Misconduct)
This common type is usually awarded when the attacker turns or gets inside the defenders and is fouled from behind. It is also recorded as a personal foul (and counted with other exclusion fouls, up to a maximum of three), even if the offence is one that normally leads to an ordinary foul.

In terms of preventing a probable goal within 6 metres, there are other situations in which this rule can be applied (leading to a penalty foul) – if a:

- defending player attempts to block a shot (or pass) with two hands;
- defending player plays the ball with a clenched fist;
- goalkeeper (or other defending player) takes the ball under the water.

There are other indications for a penalty foul alone:

- For an excluded player to interfere with play, or not leave immediately. Another exclusion (personal) foul is recorded on that player, and a penalty is awarded;
- For an excluded player to re-enter (or substitute to

enter) improperly; eg, without a signal from the referee, or not from the re-entry area. They are excluded (again) but only one personal foul is recorded. And a penalty is awarded (if the player's team is not in possession of the ball);[32]

Improper re-entry also includes lifting the rope to pass under it. So this action may also lead to a penalty (if their team is on the defensive, and if the alignment of the goal is affected). This can happen if an excluded player rushes re-entry (from the re-entry area) after possession has changed. All of these actions are easy to do in the heat of a game. But as the sanction can be quite serious (a penalty), a player is unlikely to do it again;

- Kick or strike an opponent within 6 metres (ie outside 6 metres, this would be an exclusion foul); this is even if the effect (or intent) is not sufficient for the action to be called a Misconduct or Brutality foul;
- When the coach (or any official) of the team not in possession of the ball requests a time out;
- For the coach (or any team official) or player to take any action with the intent to prevent a probable goal or delaying the game; eg a coach or substitute delaying the return of the ball. Less significant time wasting by a player can lead to an ordinary foul (see earlier);
- Brutality foul.

Penalty Foul with Misconduct
These two offences are heavily sanctioned in water polo:

- For a player (or substitute) who is not entitled to participate in the play at that time to enter the field of play; for example, if a player (or substitute) with three exclusions re-enters the pool.

---

[32] If the offence is committed by a player of the team in possession of the ball, a free throw is awarded to the opposing team.

He/she is sent off for Misconduct and a penalty is awarded;

- For the goalkeeper (or any defending player) to pull over the goal completely, with the object of preventing a probable goal. He/she is sent off for Misconduct and a penalty is awarded.

The referee signals a penalty foul in this manner: (1) long blast of the whistle; (2) five fingers held up with a raised arm; then (3) putting up one or both hands, indicating the number of the offending player.

Conduct of participants not in the water

The referee can issue yellow or red cards when the behaviour of participants not in the water (players, coaches, other team personnel, or spectators) is inappropriate.

The yellow card is reserved for the head coach and is a warning that the behaviour of someone (including the head coach) on the bench is inappropriate.[33] The yellow card may be issued at any point in the game and can be issued as a 'walking yellow', in which the referee pulls a yellow card out without stopping live play. After issuing a walking yellow, at the next stoppage of play, the referee may pull the ball out to inform both the scoring table (especially if they think that the table has not noticed the walking yellow) and the other referee, of the issuance of that card.

The red card is awarded when the behaviour is bad enough that the referee orders that person (from the bench if relevant) to leave the swimming pool area, ie for Misconduct. Someone who receives the red card may not have any visual, verbal, or electronic communication with any member of the team for the remainder of that game and all of the next game. Ie this is similar to the red card for a Brutality foul. Fortunately, red cards are few in water polo.

---

[33] The referee can issue a 'verbal warning' (ie of an impending yellow card) but this is not within the rules; they may go straight to a yellow or red card.

Chapter Seven: Referee Signals

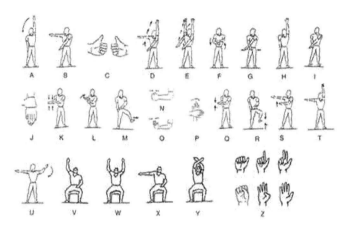

Figure 14: Referee and goal judge signals (FINA, 2017)

Fig. A How a referee signals (i) the start of the period, (ii) a restart after a goal, and (iii) the taking of a penalty throw; by lowering the arm from a vertical position. **Lower arm to start/restart game.**

Fig. B How a referee signals a free throw, goal throw or corner throw; by pointing with one arm in the direction of the attack and using the other arm to indicate the place where the ball is to be put into play. This is combined with one or two short whistles. **Point in direction of attack for free, goal or corner throw.**

Fig. C How a referee signals a neutral throw. The referee points both thumbs up and calls for the ball, and points to the place where the neutral throw has been awarded. **Two thumbs up for neutral throw (and call for ball).**

Fig. D How a referee signals the exclusion of a player (exclusion foul). The referee points to the player and then moves the arm quickly towards the team's re-entry area. Then the referee signals the excluded player's number to the scoring table. This is combined with three whistles, the last one being a long one. **Point to player then re-entry area for exclusion.**

Fig. E How a referee signals the simultaneous exclusion of two players. The referee points with both hands to the two players, signals their exclusion in accordance with Figure 14 (above), and then signals the players' cap numbers.

Fig. F How a referee signals the exclusion of a player for misconduct with substitution after 20 seconds (exclusion misconduct foul). The referee signals exclusion as shown in the figure above, ie by rotating the hands round one another in such a way that is visible to both the field of play and the scoring table. A red card is also issued. The referee then signals the excluded player's number to the scoring table. **'Saturday night fever ('wrapped')' = Misconduct.**

Fig. G How a referee signals the exclusion of a player for brutality with substitution after four minutes (exclusion brutality foul). The referee signals this type of exclusion foul with low crossed fists, in such a way that is visible to both the field of play and the table. A red card is also issued. The referee then signals the excluded player's cap number to the table. **Low crossed fists = Brutality.**

Fig. H How a referee signals the award of a penalty throw. The referee raises an arm with five fingers in the air. The referee then signals the offending player's number to the scoring table. **Raised arm with five fingers = Penalty.**

Fig. I How a referee signals a goal has been scored. The referee signals by a whistle and by pointing to the centre of the field of play. **Point towards centre of field = goal.**

Fig. J How a referee signals the exclusion foul of holding an opponent. The referee makes a motion holding the wrist of one hand with the other hand. **Holding wrist = exclusion foul for holding.**

Fig. K How a referee indicates the exclusion foul of sinking an opponent. The referee makes a downward motion with both hands starting from a horizontal position. **Two hands downward movement = exclusion foul for sinking (one hand down means an ordinary foul for ball under).**

Fig. L How a referee indicates the exclusion foul of pulling back an opponent. The referee makes a pulling motion with both hands vertically extended and pulling towards his body. **Two hands pulling motion = exclusion foul for pulling.**

Fig. M How a referee indicates the exclusion foul of kicking an opponent. The referee makes a kicking movement. **Kicking movement = exclusion foul for kicking.**

Fig. N How a referee indicates the exclusion foul of striking an opponent. The referee makes a striking motion with a closed fist starting from a horizontal position. **Horizontal striking movement with closed fist = exclusion foul for striking.**

Fig. O How a referee signals the ordinary foul of pushing or pushing off from an opponent. This may be done by an attacker, pushing off a defender, to gain space to pass or shoot. The referee makes a pushing motion away from the body starting from a horizontal position. **Horizontal pushing away = ordinary foul for pushing.**

Fig. P How a referee indicates the exclusion foul of impeding an opponent. The referee makes a crossing motion with one flat hand horizontally crossing the other. **Horizontal flat hands crossing = ordinary foul for impeding.**

Fig. Q How a referee indicates the ordinary foul of taking the ball under the water. The referee makes a downward motion with a hand starting from a horizontal position. **Downward hand = ordinary foul for ball under (two hands down is an exclusion foul for sinking).**

Fig. R How a referee indicates the ordinary foul of standing on the bottom of the pool. The referee raises and lowers one foot. **Raise one foot = ordinary foul of standing.**

Fig. S How a referee signals the ordinary foul of undue delay in the taking of a free throw, goal throw or corner throw. The referee raises a hand once or twice with the palm turned upwards. **Raise hand with palm up = ordinary foul of delay in free, goal or corner throw.**

Fig. T How a referee indicates the ordinary foul of a violation of the two-metre rule. The referee indicates the number 2 by raising the fore and middle fingers in the air with the arm vertically. **Raise two fingers (index/middle) = ordinary foul of being within 2 metres.**

Fig. U How a referee indicates the ordinary fouls of wasting time and the expiry of 30 seconds possession. The referee moves a hand in a circular motion two or three times. **Move hand in circular motion = time wasting or expiry of 30 seconds.**

Fig. V How a goal judge signals he/she is ready for the start of a period.

Fig. W How a goal judge signals an improper start, restart or improper re-entry of an excluded player or substitute.

Fig. X How a goal judge signals a goal throw or corner throw.

Fig. Y How a goal judge signals a goal.

Fig. Z How a referee indicates a player's cap number. To enable the referee to communicate better with the players and the secretary, signals are made using one or both hands (if the number exceeds five). One hand shows player numbers one to five, using that many fingers; with the other hand showing additional fingers to make up the sum of the player's number, for numbers six to nine. A clenched fist is used to show the number ten. If the number exceeds ten, one hand is shown as a clenched fist with the other hand showing additional fingers to make up the sum of the player's number.

Figure 15: After the Game

Made in the USA
Coppell, TX
19 January 2020

14694850R10039